English Master

C2 Key Word Transformation

Margaret Cooze

200 exercises for the
Cambridge C2 Proficiency

PROSPERITY EDUCATION

PROSPERITY EDUCATION
www.prosperityeducation.net

Registered offices: Sherlock Close, Cambridge
CB3 0HP, United Kingdom

© Prosperity Education Ltd. 2022

First published 2022

ISBN: 978-1-913825-65-2

This publication is in copyright. Subject to statutory exception and to the provisions of relevant collective licensing agreements, no reproduction of any part may take place without the written permission of Prosperity Education.

'Use of English', 'Cambridge C2 Proficiency' and 'CPE' are brands belonging to The Chancellor, Masters and Scholars of the University of Cambridge and are not associated with Prosperity Education or its products.

The moral rights of the author have been asserted.

For further information and resources, visit:
www.prosperityeducation.net

To infinity and beyond

Contents

Introduction	iv
Test 1	1
Test 2	5
Test 3	9
Test 4	13
Test 5	17
Test 6	21
Test 7	25
Test 8	29
Test 9	33
Test 10	37
Test 11	41
Test 12	45
Test 13	49
Test 14	53
Test 15	57
Test 16	61
Test 17	65
Test 18	69
Test 19	73
Test 20	77
Answers	81

Introduction

Welcome to this edition of sample tests for the Cambridge C2 Proficiency, Part 4: Key Word Transformation, designed specifically for students preparing for the challenging Use of English section of the (CPE) examination, but also suitable for any English language student working at CEFR C2 level.

C2 results are given against the *Cambridge English Scale*, which is the average score for the four skills and the Use of English section of the test. You will need to get a score of 200 or higher to be awarded a certificate at C2. In order to allow ample time for the reading parts (Parts 5–7) of Paper 1, it is advisable that candidates complete The Use of English section (Parts 1–4) as quickly as possible while maintaining accuracy.

This resource contains 200 exam-styled, single-sentence assessments, each carrying a lexical/lexico-grammatical focus, testing lexis, grammar and vocabulary. Each assessment comprises a sentence, followed by a 'key' word and an alternative sentence conveying the same meaning as the first but with a gap in the middle. Use the key word provided to complete the second sentence so that it has a similar meaning to the first sentence. You cannot change the keyword provided. Each correct answer is broken down into two marks. Next to each sentence transformation answer you will find a guide indicating the focus of the two parts of the answer: either G (grammatical) or L (lexical). This is a rough indication to help you with your revision for the exam. At this level, grammar and lexis are often integrated, but this device gives a rough indication to help you with your revision for the exam.

Author **Margaret Cooze** taught extensively in the UK and abroad before moving into academic management and teacher training. She holds an MA in Applied Linguistics and an MSc in English Language Teaching Management, and has worked in senior roles at Cambridge English Language Assessment and Cambridge Assessment International Education.

Visit www.prosperityeducation.net for more C2 Proficiency exam practice:

Cambridge C2 Proficiency
Use of English

Part 4

Test 1

Cambridge C2 Proficiency Use of English

Part 4 — Key word transformation — **Test 1**

For questions 1–10, complete the second sentence, using the word given, so that it has a similar meaning to the first sentence. Do not change the word provided, and use between three and eight words in total. In the separate answer sheet, write your answers in capital letters, using one box per letter.

1 Impressively, he learned to play the guitar in just six weeks.

   PICKED

   For him _____ in just six weeks is impressive.

2 Nobody seemed to know exactly how often the buses ran.

   FREQUENCY

   The _____ to be known by anybody.

3 They were never really sure that she needed to know.

   DEBATEABLE

   It _____ not she needed to know.

4 I believe he allows employees to be as creative as they like in their work.

   SCOPE

   He is understood to _____ in employee's work.

5   In her speech she didn't mention how much her assistant had contributed.

    NO

    Her speech _____ made by her assistant.

6   You'll have an accident if you put too much in each glass.

    BRIM

    If you _____ you'll have an accident.

7   I don't blame you for feeling upset about this.

    EVERY

    You _____ upset about this.

8   It's amazing that she still works in that job.

    HELD

    That she _____ amaze me.

9   Somehow, his ideas often manage to make the task more complex.

    DIMENSION

    He often _____ to the task.

10 Have the timetable revisions been seen yet?

    SIGHT

    Has anyone _____ timetable yet?

Answer sheet: Key word transformation Test No. ☐

Name _____ **Date** _____

Write your answers in capital letters, using one box per letter.

1.
2.
3.
4.
5.
6.
7.
8.
9.
10.

Mark out of 20 ☐

Cambridge C2 Proficiency
Use of English

Part 4

Test 2

Cambridge C2 Proficiency Use of English

Part 4 — Key word transformation — Test 2

For questions 1–10, complete the second sentence, using the word given, so that it has a similar meaning to the first sentence. Do not change the word provided, and use between three and eight words in total. In the separate answer sheet, write your answers in capital letters, using one box per letter.

1. It seems that she was misinformed about the route.

   INACCURATE

   She appears _____ way to go.

2. He believed that it wasn't the best thing to do.

   OPINION

   He was _____ better ideas.

3. I heard that just about everybody condemned the idea.

   WIDESPREAD

   There was _____ of the idea.

4. If they do win, then I don't think it will be by much.

   MARGIN

   Any victory will _____ in my opinion.

5 You should take full advantage of all the facilities while you're here.

   GOOD

   During _____ the facilities.

6 They shouldn't have been so abusive to him.

   TORRENT

   He shouldn't have _____ abuse from them.

7 Is he going to talk to the class about the outing in your opinion?

   MENTION

   Do you _____ of the outing to the class?

8 It all ended rather suddenly, didn't it?

   ABRUPT

   That it _____ surprised me.

9 Everyone was amazed when they saw how good he was.

   UTTER

   To _____, he was very skillful.

10 She remembered her mother taking her there.

   BEEN

   She recalled _____ her mother.

Answer sheet: Key word transformation   Test No. ☐

Name _____   **Date** _____

Write your answers in capital letters, using one box per letter.

1. ☐☐☐☐☐☐☐☐☐☐☐☐☐
   ☐☐☐☐☐☐☐☐☐☐☐☐☐

2. ☐☐☐☐☐☐☐☐☐☐☐☐☐
   ☐☐☐☐☐☐☐☐☐☐☐☐☐

3. ☐☐☐☐☐☐☐☐☐☐☐☐☐
   ☐☐☐☐☐☐☐☐☐☐☐☐☐

4. ☐☐☐☐☐☐☐☐☐☐☐☐☐
   ☐☐☐☐☐☐☐☐☐☐☐☐☐

5. ☐☐☐☐☐☐☐☐☐☐☐☐☐
   ☐☐☐☐☐☐☐☐☐☐☐☐☐

6. ☐☐☐☐☐☐☐☐☐☐☐☐☐
   ☐☐☐☐☐☐☐☐☐☐☐☐☐

7. ☐☐☐☐☐☐☐☐☐☐☐☐☐
   ☐☐☐☐☐☐☐☐☐☐☐☐☐

8. ☐☐☐☐☐☐☐☐☐☐☐☐☐
   ☐☐☐☐☐☐☐☐☐☐☐☐☐

9. ☐☐☐☐☐☐☐☐☐☐☐☐☐
   ☐☐☐☐☐☐☐☐☐☐☐☐☐

10. ☐☐☐☐☐☐☐☐☐☐☐☐☐
    ☐☐☐☐☐☐☐☐☐☐☐☐☐

Mark out of 20 ☐

Cambridge C2 Proficiency
Use of English

Part 4

Test 3

Cambridge C2 Proficiency Use of English

Part 4   Key word transformation   Test 3

For questions 1–10, complete the second sentence, using the word given, so that it has a similar meaning to the first sentence. Do not change the word provided, and use between three and eight words in total. In the separate answer sheet, write your answers in capital letters, using one box per letter.

1. When he was younger, he didn't need a single thing.

   FOR

   As _____ nothing.

2. Both twins always wanted to be better than the other.

   TRYING

   The twins _____ each other.

3. Nobody could ever have imagined such a disastrous event.

   MAGNITUDE

   A _____ imagined by anyone.

4. I am contacting you about the job you have advertised.

   REGARD

   I am making _____ the advertised job.

5 People say he desperately needs new accommodation.

DIRE

It is _____ a new place to live.

6 If they can buy that house, they must be rolling in it.

HARD

They _____ afford to buy that house.

7 I'm in total agreement with you about the plans.

WHOLE

I _____ you about the plans.

8 I'm certain the police won't have forgotten to contact him.

HAVE

The police are _____ contact with him.

9 I was thinking of asking her to design a new dress for me like she offered.

UP

I was considering _____ a new dress for me.

10 The house was spotless!

SPECK

There _____ anywhere to be seen!

Answer sheet: Key word transformation Test No.

Name _____   **Date** _____

Write your answers in capital letters, using one box per letter.

1.

2.

3.

4.

5.

6.

7.

8.

9.

10.

Mark out of 20

Cambridge C2 Proficiency Use of English

Part 4

Test 4

Cambridge C2 Proficiency Use of English

Part 4 — Key word transformation — **Test 4**

For questions 1–10, complete the second sentence, using the word given, so that it has a similar meaning to the first sentence. Do not change the word provided, and use between three and eight words in total. In the separate answer sheet, write your answers in capital letters, using one box per letter.

1. He refused to get involved when she started arguing with her father.

   DRAWN

   He wouldn't _____ with her father.

2. A fault on her phone meant that my call went unanswered.

   CAUSED

   Her _____ my call.

3. Her suggestion was a total surprise to me.

   ABACK

   I _____ she suggested.

4. I hate the way he patronises his staff.

   DOWN

   The way he _____ for him is awful.

5 What he is asking for is very confusing.

BAFFLED

I'm completely _____ is making.

6 He talked to the student about his results separately from the others.

SIDE

He _____ to tell him his results.

7 He applied for citizenship but it wasn't successful.

BECOME

His _____ was rejected.

8 Why not offer the customer a refund as the goods are faulty?

BACK

You _____ the faulty goods.

9 She managed to make the lecture last for much longer than it should have done.

OUT

She really _____ needed to be.

10 He has enough money to eat in restaurants most nights.

DINE

He's _____ every night.

Answer sheet: Key word transformation

Test No.

Name _____ **Date** _____

Write your answers in capital letters, using one box per letter.

1.
2.
3.
4.
5.
6.
7.
8.
9.
10.

Mark out of 20

Cambridge C2 Proficiency
Use of English

Part 4

Test 5

Cambridge C2 Proficiency Use of English

Part 4 Key word transformation Test 5

For questions 1–10, complete the second sentence, using the word given, so that it has a similar meaning to the first sentence. Do not change the word provided, and use between three and eight words in total. In the separate answer sheet, write your answers in capital letters, using one box per letter.

1 I think that they have looked at the proposal again and have reduced the equipment.

SCALED

The equipment _____, I believe.

2 Janet said that it was just possible that we would travel to London.

OUT

Travelling to London _____ by Janet.

3 When I arrived at the house, they were arguing very loudly about the arrangements for the party.

BLAZING

Arriving at the house, _____ about the party arrangements.

4 I wonder why she decided to miss the meeting.

EXCUSE

I'd like _____ the meeting was.

5 She told me that he was reducing his working hours.

BACK

He is _____ he works.

6 It's time we told them we are going home.

OUR

We should _____ and leave.

7 You don't have to go to the meeting if you don't want to

UNDER

You _____ to go to the meeting.

8 She thanked him for his help, and then didn't talk to him again all evening!

BY

After being _____ all evening.

9 She is being pressurised to quit her job.

GROWING

There _____ in her resignation.

10 After they left, the precious document was never seen again.

WITHOUT

The precious document _____ departure.

Answer sheet: Key word transformation Test No. ☐

Name _____   **Date** _____

Write your answers in capital letters, using one box per letter.

1.
2.
3.
4.
5.
6.
7.
8.
9.
10.

Mark out of 20 ☐

Cambridge C2 Proficiency
Use of English

Part 4

Test 6

Cambridge C2 Proficiency Use of English

Part 4 — Key word transformation — **Test 6**

For questions 1–10, complete the second sentence, using the word given, so that it has a similar meaning to the first sentence. Do not change the word provided, and use between three and eight words in total. In the separate answer sheet, write your answers in capital letters, using one box per letter.

1. Someone is mending that old sewing machine just now.

    REPAIR

    That old sewing machine _____ moment.

2. The original plan was to demolish the old factory when they had enough money.

    DUE

    The old factory _____ afford it.

3. I don't think this situation is as important as you think it is.

    READING

    I think you _____ this situation.

4. If I were you, I would ask a lawyer how much the company is worth.

    ADVICE

    You should _____ value.

5 I was expecting the test results last Friday.

DAY

Last Friday _____ due.

6 We're not obliged to give a refund.

UNDER

We _____ customer's money.

7 Not many people know that they are going to move.

KNOWN

It _____ the cards.

8 From looking at her you would think she didn't care about anything.

LIKE

She acts _____ world.

9 If you want to question anything, please do.

FREE

Anyone who wants _____ do so.

10 Our final act was to load the car.

DID

The last _____ in the car.

Answer sheet: Key word transformation Test No. ☐

Name _____ **Date** _____

Write your answers in capital letters, using one box per letter.

1.
2.
3.
4.
5.
6.
7.
8.
9.
10.

Mark out of 20 ☐

Cambridge C2 Proficiency
Use of English

Part 4

Test 7

Cambridge C2 Proficiency Use of English

Part 4 Key word transformation Test 7

For questions 1–10, complete the second sentence, using the word given, so that it has a similar meaning to the first sentence. Do not change the word provided, and use between three and eight words in total. In the separate answer sheet, write your answers in capital letters, using one box per letter.

1 It's very possible that he will change his mind.

   DISTINCT

   There _____ a change of opinion.

2 She will find some way to avoid having to do her share of the work.

   WRIGGLE

   She is _____ doing her part of the task.

3 I suppose it's possible that he will arrive before the presentation starts.

   CONCEIVABLY

   He _____ for the presentation.

4 That's why we have exactly the same amount of money as you did.

   RICHER

   That's the _____ you were.

5 I don't think they are interested in visiting other cities.

NO

They _____ to offer.

6 I don't think you understand what she is trying to say about the homework.

POINT

You seem _____ we have to do for homework.

7 She made a change of great significance to the performance of the team.

HUGELY

Her _____ for the team's performance.

8 The nutrition in fast-food meals can be just as high as in other foods.

BIT

Fast food _____ other foods.

9 I've heard that she notices everything so be careful!

BALL

The word is _____ care!

10 They were exhausted but they continued until they completed the job.

PRESSED

Despite _____ was complete.

Answer sheet: Key word transformation Test No. ☐

Name _____ **Date** _____

Write your answers in capital letters, using one box per letter.

1.
2.
3.
4.
5.
6.
7.
8.
9.
10.

Mark out of 20 ☐

Cambridge C2 Proficiency
Use of English

Part 4

Test 8

Cambridge C2 Proficiency Use of English

Part 4   Key word transformation   Test 8

For questions 1–10, complete the second sentence, using the word given, so that it has a similar meaning to the first sentence. Do not change the word provided, and use between three and eight words in total. In the separate answer sheet, write your answers in capital letters, using one box per letter.

1. It's very unusual to hear of foxes being spotted in the city centre.

   ALMOST

   It's _____ seen in the centre of the city.

2. I'm always surprised by how many unwanted things arrive in the post every day.

   REGULARITY

   I get junk _____ each day.

3. I'm relieved to know that her school work is getting much better.

   MARKED

   Her school work _____, which is a relief.

4. She never stops telling people that her son in a gifted artist.

   BOASTING

   She _____ talent.

5 In his role, it's his job is to keep standards up.

   RESPONSIBILITY

   It is _____ standards at the factory.

6 Do you think it would be possible to finish this before Friday?

   OF

   Is there _____ completed by Friday.

7 We eventually discovered that we were never going to be allowed to join the club.

   OUT

   Trying to join the club _____ of time.

8 It isn't always easy to get reliable wifi, so don't rely on being able to get online.

   OF

   You shouldn't depend _____ the patchy wifi.

9 There has been a lot of discussion about these issues over the past few years.

   WIDELY

   These issues _____ times.

10 It wasn't very sensible of me to expect that she would help with the project.

   BETTER

   I _____ to help with the project.

Answer sheet: Key word transformation Test No. ☐

Name _____ **Date** _____

Write your answers in capital letters, using one box per letter.

1.
2.
3.
4.
5.
6.
7.
8.
9.
10.

Mark out of 20 ☐

Cambridge C2 Proficiency
Use of English

Part 4

Test 9

Cambridge C2 Proficiency Use of English

Part 4 Key word transformation Test 9

For questions 1–10, complete the second sentence, using the word given, so that it has a similar meaning to the first sentence. Do not change the word provided, and use between three and eight words in total. In the separate answer sheet, write your answers in capital letters, using one box per letter.

1 I don't think we can expect them to come all this way for such a short meeting.

OF

It's asking _____ far just for a short meeting I think.

2 If it wasn't for his determination, he would have resigned.

EMPLOYED

He would no _____ less determined.

3 They are widely believed to have stolen the items.

OPINION

Nearly everyone _____ the robbery.

4 He would prefer not to have to pay for his ticket at all!

WOULD

His _____ be free!

5 His leadership skills are excellent, so this job is perfect for him.

   BORN

   He is a _____ his street.

6 Do you think you could close all of the windows in the building?

   AS

   Would you _____ window in the building?

7 Nobody listened to her to despite her attempts to tell everyone what to do.

   LAY

   She was _____ ignored her.

8 Only employees are allowed to enter the building.

   RESTRICTED

   Entry _____ who work here.

9 Touching those wires is a very silly thing to do.

   UNWISE

   You'd _____ those wires.

10 What would you do if you couldn't work here?

    OF

    Suppose _____ here, what would you do?

Answer sheet: Key word transformation Test No. ☐

Name _____ **Date** _____

Write your answers in capital letters, using one box per letter.

1.

2.

3.

4.

5.

6.

7.

8.

9.

10.

Mark out of 20 ☐

Cambridge C2 Proficiency
Use of English

Part 4

Test 10

Cambridge C2 Proficiency Use of English

Part 4 — Key word transformation — **Test 10**

For questions 1–10, complete the second sentence, using the word given, so that it has a similar meaning to the first sentence. Do not change the word provided, and use between three and eight words in total. In the separate answer sheet, write your answers in capital letters, using one box per letter.

1 Ever since he lost his job, he's had so much bad luck.

DOGGED

He's _____ made redundant.

2 It's quite likely that he'll get lost.

FAIR

There's _____ way.

3 I didn't think the job would suit him!

DOUBTS

I had _____ the job.

4 Nobody should have forced you to do something you didn't want to.

COMPELLED

You never _____ something you didn't want to.

5 I'm pretty sure that it'll rain tomorrow.

   REMOTE

   There's _____ weather tomorrow.

6 She was sent to prison when they agreed she had committed the crime.

   FOUND

   Having been _____ up.

7 You need to concentrate on this as it's an important thing to understand.

   GRASPING

   Pay _____ is important.

8 I go to the gym fairly frequently.

   EVERY

   I make _____ again.

9 I expect the water will be the same temperature as it was yesterday.

   BELIEVE

   There's no _____ warmer than it was yesterday.

10 I'm sure I don't need to tell you about the importance of the rules.

   WITHOUT

   It _____ follow the rules.

Answer sheet: Key word transformation   Test No.

Name _____   **Date** _____

Write your answers in capital letters, using one box per letter.

1.

2.

3.

4.

5.

6.

7.

8.

9.

10.

Mark out of 20

Cambridge C2 Proficiency
Use of English

Part 4

Test 11

Cambridge C2 Proficiency Use of English

Part 4   Key word transformation   Test 11

For questions 1–10, complete the second sentence, using the word given, so that it has a similar meaning to the first sentence. Do not change the word provided, and use between three and eight words in total. In the separate answer sheet, write your answers in capital letters, using one box per letter.

1. You should be proud of passing your driving test.

   TAKE

   Passing your driving test _____ in.

2. What annoyed the workers was that the management never consulted them.

   ALIENATED

   It was the lack _____ the management.

3. You'll only get significantly better if you do regular practice.

   REGULARLY

   Only by _____ progress

4. I fail to understand my friends' views on the matter.

   BEYOND

   I have some _____ me.

5 You shouldn't overstate the results of the test.

   MUCH

   Don't place _____ of the test.

6 The possible outcome fills me with horror.

   WOULD

   I dread _____ happened.

7 I suppose we will all have electric cars eventually.

   COMMON

   I dare _____ the end.

8 You should leave now or you could miss your flight.

   RUN

   You _____ you don't leave now.

9 I've only just realised that someone has stolen my passport at the airport.

   DAWNED

   It's just _____ stolen at the airport.

10 I have never seen such a bad film.

   RANK

   This _____ ever made.

Answer sheet: Key word transformation Test No. ☐

Name _____ **Date** _____

Write your answers in capital letters, using one box per letter.

1.
2.
3.
4.
5.
6.
7.
8.
9.
10.

Mark out of 20 ☐

Cambridge C2 Proficiency
Use of English

Part 4

Test 12

Cambridge C2 Proficiency Use of English

Part 4 — Key word transformation — **Test 12**

For questions 1–10, complete the second sentence, using the word given, so that it has a similar meaning to the first sentence. Do not change the word provided, and use between three and eight words in total. In the separate answer sheet, write your answers in capital letters, using one box per letter.

1 They said that every suggestion I made was unrealistic for the project.

DISMISSED

All _____ being unrealistic for the project.

2 I am shocked that so many species may become extinct.

FACING

The fact that such _____ is shocking.

3 In spite of being married for so many years, they agreed to end it.

DAY

They decided _____ marriage.

4 After he resigned as manager, there were lots of problems with the accuracy of orders.

STOOD

The accuracy of orders was _____ as manager.

5 People often resist new ideas.

EMBRACED

New ideas _____ resistance.

6 You wouldn't believe how often I've wanted to hand in my notice.

TIME

There's _____ I could quit my job.

7 If she hadn't been so brave, I think the boat would have been lost.

HER

But _____ boat would have been found.

8 The two football teams are very competitive it's still friendly.

RIVALRY

There _____ the two teams.

9 All travellers must have a passport.

OBLIGATORY

Possession _____ for any passenger.

10 After she presented at the meeting, everyone thought she should get the job.

FRONTRUNNER

She emerged _____ presentation at the meeting.

Answer sheet: Key word transformation Test No. ☐

Name _____ **Date** _____

Write your answers in capital letters, using one box per letter.

1.
2.
3.
4.
5.
6.
7.
8.
9.
10.

Mark out of 20 ☐

Cambridge C2 Proficiency
Use of English

Part 4

Test 13

Cambridge C2 Proficiency Use of English

Part 4   Key word transformation   Test 13

For questions 1–10, complete the second sentence, using the word given, so that it has a similar meaning to the first sentence. Do not change the word provided, and use between three and eight words in total. In the separate answer sheet, write your answers in capital letters, using one box per letter.

1   You should prioritise accepting the truth.

FACTS

You really need _____ priority.

2   It was quickly clear that she could persuade anyone.

POWERS

Her _____ apparent.

3   I admit that I know nothing at all about the subject.

CONFESS

I have _____ ignorant on the subject.

4   I'm not sure whether to accept to the job offer.

MINDS

I'm in _____ offered me.

5 I can get by in Spanish but speak Italian fluently.

KNOWLEDGE

I have _____ in Italian.

6 I am certain he lied about his experience.

FACT

I know _____ lies about his experience.

7 It's hard not to eat chocolate as I've always loved sweet things.

TOOTH

Having _____ by chocolate.

8 We had hoped that the bus service would be more reliable.

PROVED

The bus service _____ we had hoped.

9 There was an amazing firework display at the end of the party.

CULMINATION

I was _____ the party.

10 They tried to stay together at the end of the race but it was chaos.

STICK

It was too _____ when they finished the race.

Answer sheet: Key word transformation   Test No. ☐

Name _____   **Date** _____

Write your answers in capital letters, using one box per letter.

1.

2.

3.

4.

5.

6.

7.

8.

9.

10.

Mark out of 20 ☐

Cambridge C2 Proficiency
Use of English

Part 4

Test 14

Cambridge C2 Proficiency Use of English

Part 4 — Key word transformation — Test 14

For questions 1–10, complete the second sentence, using the word given, so that it has a similar meaning to the first sentence. Do not change the word provided, and use between three and eight words in total. In the separate answer sheet, write your answers in capital letters, using one box per letter.

1 She craved attention when she was a child.

   CENTRE

   She always wanted _____ child.

2 Fortunately, there were no casualties in last night's accident.

   UNSCATHED

   It was _____ accident last night.

3 As she knows the city so well, she never loses her way.

   HAND

   She knows the city like _____ lost.

4 We should all contribute, then we'll have plenty of money.

   CLUBS

   If _____ than enough.

5 There has been a dramatic fall in orders in the past twelve months.

TIME

Since _____ dramatically.

6 I know it's not important, but it's clear that this is not his car.

IMPORTANCE

It's _____ isn't his.

7 There's no point in asking him for help.

TIME

It's _____ from him.

8 I used to find it completely impossible to understand what she said.

TAIL

I couldn't _____ she said.

9 I must say that thinking about the interview tomorrow is making me nervous.

ADMIT

I have _____ interview is making me nervous.

10 There were rumours that he was on his sixth marriage!

BE

He _____ six times!

Answer sheet: Key word transformation Test No. ☐

Name _____ **Date** _____

Write your answers in capital letters, using one box per letter.

1. ▢▢▢▢▢▢▢▢▢▢▢▢▢
2. ▢▢▢▢▢▢▢▢▢▢▢▢▢
3. ▢▢▢▢▢▢▢▢▢▢▢▢▢
4. ▢▢▢▢▢▢▢▢▢▢▢▢▢
5. ▢▢▢▢▢▢▢▢▢▢▢▢▢
6. ▢▢▢▢▢▢▢▢▢▢▢▢▢
7. ▢▢▢▢▢▢▢▢▢▢▢▢▢
8. ▢▢▢▢▢▢▢▢▢▢▢▢▢
9. ▢▢▢▢▢▢▢▢▢▢▢▢▢
10. ▢▢▢▢▢▢▢▢▢▢▢▢▢

Mark out of 20 ☐

Cambridge C2 Proficiency
Use of English

Part 4

Test 15

Cambridge C2 Proficiency Use of English

Part 4   Key word transformation   **Test 15**

For questions 1–10, complete the second sentence, using the word given, so that it has a similar meaning to the first sentence. Do not change the word provided, and use between three and eight words in total. In the separate answer sheet, write your answers in capital letters, using one box per letter.

1. When these things happen, you learn who you can rely on.

   THIS

   It's at _____ your true friends are.

2. Only last week did I see the same thing.

   THAN

   I _____ week ago.

3. Her artwork surprised me by how beautiful it was.

   SHEER

   I was blown _____ of her artwork.

4. That she didn't object to the proposed changes was rather surprising.

   BLESSING

   I was somewhat _____ the proposal.

5 I really don't think you should change your mind.

GUNS

You should _____ ask me.

6 No doubt there were many complaints when the mistake was discovered.

CAME

Many people _____ light.

7 They insisted that they hadn't made a mistake.

ADAMANT

They _____ made by them.

8 In his opinion, nobody was as good as he was at tennis.

REGARDED

He never _____ as him at tennis.

9 I wasn't surprised at all that so many people attended the meeting.

CROWD

That _____ as little surprise.

10 Sometimes you have to be strict when children behave badly.

FOOT

When children _____ on occasions.

Answer sheet: Key word transformation Test No.

Name _____   **Date** _____

Write your answers in capital letters, using one box per letter.

1.
2.
3.
4.
5.
6.
7.
8.
9.
10.

Mark out of 20

Cambridge C2 Proficiency Use of English

Part 4

Test 16

Cambridge C2 Proficiency Use of English

Part 4 — Key word transformation — Test 16

For questions 1–10, complete the second sentence, using the word given, so that it has a similar meaning to the first sentence. Do not change the word provided, and use between three and eight words in total. In the separate answer sheet, write your answers in capital letters, using one box per letter.

1. Our success depends on making sure everything has been done.

   CHANCE

   We can't _____ to be successful.

2. My kitchen really needs to be repainted.

   BENEFIT

   What my kitchen _____ again.

3. I am doubtful that she is enthusiastic about the role.

   OPEN

   Her enthusiasm _____ doubt in my opinion.

4. Unfortunately, they neglected to check the paperwork.

   WERE

   That _____ paperwork was unfortunate.

5 I don't think that we will meet again.

   PATHS

   It's highly _____ again.

6 That he is the strongest applicant is obvious.

   SAYING

   It _____ is the strongest.

7 His objections to the plans were totally justified.

   RIGHT

   He had _____ the plans

8 It wasn't surprising that everyone was silent when he asked the question.

   WALL

   His question _____, which wasn't surprising.

9 I can't say as I am looking forward to helping her to find a job!

   PROSPECT

   I don't _____ her job search!

10 She's certainly no longer my friend after betraying me so blatantly.

   NO

   After that _____ mine any more.

Answer sheet: Key word transformation Test No.

Name _____ **Date** _____

Write your answers in capital letters, using one box per letter.

1.
2.
3.
4.
5.
6.
7.
8.
9.
10.

Mark out of 20

Cambridge C2 Proficiency Use of English

Part 4

Test 17

Cambridge C2 Proficiency Use of English

Part 4 — Key word transformation — Test 17

For questions 1–10, complete the second sentence, using the word given, so that it has a similar meaning to the first sentence. Do not change the word provided, and use between three and eight words in total. In the separate answer sheet, write your answers in capital letters, using one box per letter.

1. She couldn't be persuaded to accept his invitation.

   INDUCE

   Nothing _____ up on his invitation.

2. Since last month, it looks as if his weight has increased.

   HAVE

   He _____ weight since last month.

3. If we had been given the right directions, we would know where we are now.

   NOW

   We would _____ been misdirected.

4. Could I ask you to clarify that last point you made?

   GIVE

   I'd be _____ on your last point.

5 It was astonishing that he wasn't beaten by anyone.

TURN

In an _____ to beat him.

6 At the noisy meeting, their feelings were made clear.

VOICED

They _____ was noisy.

7 I didn't think this was her first visit there.

UNDER

I _____ there before.

8 We agreed to disagree as it was possible that the job wouldn't be finished on time.

ASIDE

We _____ the job got finished on time.

9 She really wanted someone to buy her that necklace for her birthday.

BEING

She had set _____ that necklace for her birthday.

10 There was outrage after the results of the election because of fraud.

PUBLIC

Due to _____ outraged.

Answer sheet: Key word transformation Test No. ☐

Name _____ **Date** _____

Write your answers in capital letters, using one box per letter.

1.
2.
3.
4.
5.
6.
7.
8.
9.
10.

Mark out of 20 ☐

Cambridge C2 Proficiency
Use of English

Part 4

Test 18

Cambridge C2 Proficiency Use of English

Part 4 — Key word transformation — **Test 18**

For questions 1–10, complete the second sentence, using the word given, so that it has a similar meaning to the first sentence. Do not change the word provided, and use between three and eight words in total. In the separate answer sheet, write your answers in capital letters, using one box per letter.

1 Occasionally he makes a bad mistake.

   WHILE

   Every _____ up badly.

2 I don't think I can make a decision until the reasons are made public.

   OPEN

   Once the reasons for the decision are _____ to make a decision.

3 She didn't say the same thing before the meeting yesterday.

   ODDS

   What she said _____ to yesterday's meeting.

4 They decided to ignore his remarks, which they found was a mistake.

   EYE

   Turning _____ out to be a mistake.

5 He took every possible step so as not to give an answer to the question.

   POWER

   He did _____ answering the question.

6 I was lucky enough to visit Laos before it got really popular as a destination.

   FORTUNE

   I had the _____ rose as a destination.

7 She used to always say that their pizza couldn't be bettered.

   SHOULDERS

   She always said _____ anyone else's.

8 My feeling was that he was overconfident.

   FULL

   I've always _____ himself.

9 I don't think it will hit home until it's right in front of us.

   SEE

   We won't believe _____ eyes, I think.

10 Since he was made redundant, he is always to trying to show everyone what he can do.

   SOMETHING

   After losing _____ to everyone.

Answer sheet: Key word transformation   Test No. ☐

Name _____   **Date** _____

Write your answers in capital letters, using one box per letter.

1.
2.
3.
4.
5.
6.
7.
8.
9.
10.

Mark out of 20 ☐

Cambridge C2 Proficiency
Use of English

Part 4

Test 19

Cambridge C2 Proficiency Use of English

Part 4 Key word transformation Test 19

For questions 1–10, complete the second sentence, using the word given, so that it has a similar meaning to the first sentence. Do not change the word provided, and use between three and eight words in total. In the separate answer sheet, write your answers in capital letters, using one box per letter.

1 I'm really not sure what to do next.

   LOSS

   I'm slightly _____ to proceed.

2 Eventually we discovered that they said no to each applicant.

   TRANSPIRED

   In the _____ down all of the applicants.

3 A lot of residents opposed the building plans last year.

   FACED

   The plans for _____ year ago.

4 If we repaint that wall in a dark colour, nobody will see what a mess it is!

   MULTITUDE

   We could _____ repainting that wall in a dark colour!

5 My sister and I are completely different.

NOTHING

I have _____ my sister.

6 In this competition, their team is doing so much worse than ours!

MILES

Our _____ in this competition.

7 So many arguments might persuade people to support her perspective.

ARGUEMENTS

There _____ of view.

8 He couldn't run as fast as others so didn't get into the team.

PACE

His omission from the team was due _____ others.

9 She didn't say anything as she was scared of saying something embarrassing.

FEAR

She didn't _____ in it.

10 Do you think you can change his mind about how to vote?

SWAY

Is it possible _____ way to vote?

Answer sheet: Key word transformation Test No.

Name _____ **Date** _____

Write your answers in capital letters, using one box per letter.

1.

2.

3.

4.

5.

6.

7.

8.

9.

10.

Mark out of 20

Cambridge C2 Proficiency Use of English

Part 4

Test 20

Cambridge C2 Proficiency Use of English

Part 4 — Key word transformation — **Test 20**

For questions 1–10, complete the second sentence, using the word given, so that it has a similar meaning to the first sentence. Do not change the word provided, and use between three and eight words in total. In the separate answer sheet, write your answers in capital letters, using one box per letter.

1. She is very proud of being able to speak Japanese fluently.

   PRIDE

   She _____ fluent in Japanese.

2. Obviously, he didn't tell the truth when he applied for the job.

   PACK

   It seems _____ on his job application.

3. You do realise you'll have to make your mind up eventually?

   FENCE

   You _____ for ever you know.

4. I really can't decide how I should manage his ideas.

   QUANDARY

   I'm _____ I should deal with his ideas.

5 The job advertisement attracted over ninety applicants.

   THAN

   No _____ the job.

6 He didn't phone last night and that made me furious.

   WAS

   What _____ me last night.

7 Nobody had expected him to donate to the fund so generously.

   SURPRISE

   Everyone _____ to the fund.

8 It's highly unlikely that she'll be promoted this year.

   HER

   There is very _____ promotion this year.

9 Honestly, I didn't think of that.

   CROSSED

   If I'm _____ mind.

10 I don't think that any of the other runners will be anywhere near as good as he is.

   SPOTS

   It's my opinion _____ all of the other runners.

Answer sheet: Key word transformation Test No. ☐

Name _____   **Date** _____

Write your answers in capital letters, using one box per letter.

1.
2.
3.
4.
5.
6.
7.
8.
9.
10.

Mark out of 20 ☐

Answers

Answers   Cambridge C2 Proficiency Use of English   Test 1

1	to have	picked up the guitar	G	L
2	exact frequency of (the) buses	didn't seem	L	G
3	was debatable (as to)	whether or not	G	G
4	allow great scope	for creativity	L	G
5	made no reference	to the contribution(s)	G	L
6	fill each glass	to the brim	L	L
7	have every right/reason	to feel	L	G
8	has held onto the/her/that job	continues to	L	G
9	manages to add/bring	a new/an extra dimension	G	L
10	had sight of	the revised/the revisions to the	G	L

Answers   Cambridge C2 Proficiency Use of English   Test 2

1	to have been given	inaccurate information about the	G	G
2	of the opinion	(that) there were	L	G
3	said to be	widespread condemnation	G	L
4	will be (achieved/won) by	a narrow/fine margin	G	L
5	your stay/visit	make good use of	L	L
6	had to take	such a torrent of	G	L
7	think he is going to	make mention	G	L
8	came to such	an abrupt end/ending	G	L
9	everyone's	utter amazement	G	L
10	having been	taken there by	G	G

Answers   Cambridge C2 Proficiency Use of English   Test 3

1	a child	he wanted for	L	L
2	were always trying	to outdo	G	L
3	disaster of this/such magnitude	could never have been	L	G
4	contact with you	with regard to	L	L
5	said (that) he is	in dire need of	G	L
6	can't be hard up	if they can	L	G
7	whole-heartedly	agree with	L	L
8	sure to have remembered	to make	G	L
9	taking her up on	her offer to design / her offer of designing	L	L
10	wasn't a speck	of dust	L	L

Answers   Cambridge C2 Proficiency Use of English   Test 4

1	be/get drawn into	her argument	L	L
2	faulty phone	caused her to miss / not to answer	L	G
3	was taken aback	by what	L	G
4	talks down to	the people who work	L	G
5	baffled by	the request he	L	L
6	took the student	to one side	L	L
7	application to become	a citizen	G	L
8	should/could give/offer the customer	their money back for	G	L
9	dragged out the lecture / dragged the lecture out	to/for longer than it	G	G
10	rich enough	to dine out/in restaurants almost/nearly	G	L

Answers — Cambridge C2 Proficiency Use of English — Test 5

1	that they proposed	has been scaled back	G	L
2	wasn't totally	ruled out	G	L
3	I found they were having / I heard them having	a blazing row	G	L
4	to know what	her excuse for missing	L	G
5	said to be	cutting back on the hours/time	G	L
6	make	our excuses	L	L
7	are under	no obligation	G	L
8	thanked by her	he was ignored	L	G
9	is growing pressure	on her to hand/give	L	G
10	disappeared/vanished without trace	after their	L	G

Answers — Cambridge C2 Proficiency Use of English — Test 6

1	is under repair	at the	L	G
2	was due to be demolished	when they could	G	G
3	are reading	too much into	L	L
4	get/take (some) legal advice	about the company's	L	G
5	was the day when	the test results were	G	G
6	are under no obligation	to return/refund (the)	L	L
7	isn't widely known	that moving (house) is on	L	L
8	like she hasn't	a care in the	G	L
9	to ask a question / question anything	should feel free to / is free to	G	L
10	thing we did	was put everything	G	L

Answers — Cambridge C2 Proficiency Use of English — Test 7

1	is a distinct possibility	that he'll have	L	G
2	sure/certain/bound to	wriggle out of	G	L
3	might/may/could conceivably	be on time	L	L
4	reason we are	no richer than	G	G
5	show/have no interest	in what other cities have	L	G
6	to be missing the point / to have missed the point	about what	L	G
7	change was	hugely significant	G	L
8	can be every bit	as nutritional as	L	G
9	she is (very) on the ball	so take	L	G
10	being exhausted they	pressed on until the job	G	L

Answers — Cambridge C2 Proficiency Use of English — Test 8

1	almost unheard of	for foxes to be	L	G
2	mail with	surprising regularity	L	L
3	is showing	a marked improvement	G	L
4	is always boasting	about her son's artistic	G	L
5	his responsibility	to maintain	L	L
6	any chance of	this being / having this	L	G
7	turned out to be	a waste	L	L
8	on being able to	get online because of	G	G
9	have been widely discussed	in recent	G	L
10	should have known better	than to expect her	G	L

Answers — Cambridge C2 Proficiency Use of English — Test 9

#				
1	too much/ a lot of them	to come so/this	L	G
2	longer be employed here	if he had been / had he been	L	G
3	is of the opinion	(that) they carried out	G	L
4	preference would be	for his ticket to	L	G
5	born leader so	this job is right up	L	L
6	be so kind as to	close each/every	L	G
7	trying to lay down the law	but everyone	L	G
8	to the building	is restricted to only those	L	G
9	be very unwise	to touch	L	G
10	you were	incapable of working	G	L

Answers — Cambridge C2 Proficiency Use of English — Test 10

#				
1	been dogged by	bad luck since he was	G	G
2	a fair chance	that he'll lose his / of him losing his	L	G
3	my doubts about / my doubts	his suitability for / that he was suitable for	L	L
4	should have been	compelled to do	G	G
5	a remote possibility/chance	of dry	L	L
6	found guilty of the crime	she was locked	L	G
7	attention to this	as grasping it clearly	L	L
8	use of the gym / trips to the gym	every now and	L	L
9	reason to believe	(that) the water will be	L	G
10	goes without saying	that you must/should/have to	L	G

Answers — Cambridge C2 Proficiency Use of English — Test 11

1	is something	to take pride / you should take pride	G	L
2	of consultation	that alienated the workers against/from	G	G
3	practising regularly	will you make significant	G	G
4	friends whose views	are beyond	G	L
5	too much emphasis	on the results	L	L
6	to think	what would have	L	G
7	say electric cars	will be/become common in	L	G
8	run the risk of missing	your/the flight if	L	G
9	dawned on me that	my passport has been	L	G
10	must rank as	the worst film	L	G

Answers — Cambridge C2 Proficiency Use of English — Test 12

1	(of) my suggestions	were dismissed as	G	G
2	a large number of species	are facing extinction	L	L
3	to call it a day	despite their long	L	L
4	problematic after	he stood down	L	L
5	are rarely/not often embraced	without (some)	G	L
6	many a time	that I've wished	L	G
7	for her bravery	I don't think the	L	G
8	is a lot of	friendly rivalry between	G	L
9	of a passport	is obligatory	L	G
10	as the frontrunner	after/following her/the	L	G

Answers   Cambridge C2 Proficiency Use of English   Test 13

1	to face the facts	as a	L	L
2	powers of persuasion	quickly became / were quickly/soon	L	G
3	to confess to	being completely/totally	G	G
4	two minds about	accepting the job (which) they	L	G
5	a working knowledge of Spanish	but am fluent	L	G
6	for a fact	(that) he told	L	G
7	a sweet tooth	I am always tempted	L	G
8	proved to be	less reliable than	G	G
9	amazed by the fireworks	at the culmination of	G	L
10	chaotic for them	to stick together	L	L

Answers   Cambridge C2 Proficiency Use of English   Test 14

1	to be the centre of attention	as a	L	G
2	fortunate that everyone/everybody	was unscathed in the	G	L
3	the back of her hand	so never gets	L	G
4	everyone/everybody clubs in/together	we'll have more	L	G
5	this time last year	orders have fallen	L	G
6	of no importance but	the car clearly	L	G
7	a waste of time	asking for help	L	G
8	make head nor tail	of anything	L	L
9	to admit that	the thought of tomorrow's / thinking about tomorrow's	L	L
10	was rumoured	to have been married	G	G

Answers Cambridge C2 Proficiency Use of English Test 15

1	moments/times like this	that you realise/learn who	L	L
2	saw the same thing	no more than a	G	G
3	away by	the sheer beauty	L	L
4	surprised that	she gave her blessing to	G	L
5	stick to your guns	if you	L	L
6	must have complained	when the mistake came to	G	L
7	were adamant (that)	the mistake hadn't been	G	G
8	regarded anyone/anybody	as being as good	L	G
9	the meeting attracted/drew	such a crowd came	G	L
10	misbehave you have to	put your foot down	G	L

Answers Cambridge C2 Proficiency Use of English Test 16

1	leave anything to chance	if we are/want	G	G
2	would benefit from	being painted	L	G
3	for the role	is (still) open to	L	L
4	they were neglectful	in checking the	G	L
5	unlikely (that)	our paths will cross	L	L
6	goes without saying	that his application	L	L
7	every right	to object to	L	G
8	was met with	a wall of silence	L	L
9	relish the prospect	of helping with	L	L
10	blatant betrayal	she's no friend of	L	L

Answers — Cambridge C2 Proficiency Use of English — Test 17

1	could induce her	to take him	L	L
2	appears/seems to have	put on / gained	G	L
3	not be lost now	if we hadn't / had we not	G	G
4	grateful if you could	give me/provide clarification	L	L
5	astonishing turn of events	nobody managed	L	L
6	voiced their feelings clearly	at the meeting which	L	G
7	was under the impression	(that) she'd been	L	G
8	put aside our differences	to ensure/make sure (that) / so that / to get	L	L
9	her heart on	being given/bought/receiving	L	G
10	the fraudulent election results / electoral fraud	the public was	L	L

Answers — Cambridge C2 Proficiency Use of English — Test 18

1	once in a while	he slips/messes	L	L
2	out in the open / open to scrutiny	I'll be/feel able	L	G
3	was at odds with	what she said prior	L	G
4	a blind eye to	his remarks turned	L	L
5	everything in his power	to avoid	L	G
6	good fortune to visit Laos	before its popularity	L	G
7	that their pizza	was head and shoulders above	G	L
8	felt (that) he was	very/extremely/too full of	L	L
9	it until we see it	with our own	G	L
10	his job he always	has something to prove	G	L

Answers Cambridge C2 Proficiency Use of English Test 19

1	at a loss	about how	L	G
2	end it transpired	that they turned	L	L
3	the building faced	a lot of opposition a	L	L
4	hide a multitude	of sins by	L	L
5	nothing in	common with	L	L
6	team is miles ahead	of theirs	L	G
7	are numerous persuasive arguments	supporting/that support her point	L	G
8	to his inability	to keep pace with	L	L
9	say anything for fear of	putting her foot	L	L
10	you could/to sway his opinion	on which / about	L	G

Answers Cambridge C2 Proficiency Use of English Test 20

1	takes great pride	in being (so/very)	L	G
2	obvious that he told	a pack of lies	G	L
3	can't	sit on the fence	G	L
4	in a (bit of a) quandary	about how	L	G
5	fewer than	ninety people applied for	L	G
6	infuriated me was / made me furious was	that he didn't call/phone	L	G
7	was taken by surprise	by the/his generous donation	L	L
8	little chance of her	being given	L	G
9	honest the idea	never crossed my	L	L
10	that he'll	knock the spots off	G	L

Notes

Notes

Notes

Notes

Notes